Mélange

Poetry by Duane Robert Pierson

Copyright © Duane Robert Pierson, 2013

All rights reserved under International and Pan-American Copyright Conventions

Printed in the United States of America

Library of Congress Control Number: 2013918994

ISBN: 978-1-4675-9101-0

Book design and layout by Nancy Bush, Violette Graphics & Printng

Copy Editing by Lesli Pike

Cover art by Nancy Bush

A special thank you to Chris Bowe of Longfellow Books for his continued support.

INTEGRITAS PUBLISHING
211 Cumberland Avenue, Apt. 510
Portland, Maine 04101
integritaspublishing@maine.rr.com
www.integritaspublishing.com

To Katie

Readers -

This is an eclectic selection of poetry. Subject matter varies considerably. Off to the side I always have a folder of poems awaiting publication. Some are recently composed. For one reason or another some poems have never been published, while others require continual reworking and polishing, so they are held until they are just right. Alas, there are a few poems that I can never quite get perfect.

It is interesting that a poet saves some poems and cannot recall as to why they were written or from whence they came. As an example this selection contains a poem titled *Martha*. I cannot recall the person with whom I was so smitten, yet I do like the poem. It has languished within my hold folder for years and finally it has been freed.

This volume has been difficult to compile. Usually my poetry books have a central theme, however with this selection that is not possible. I have attempted to open this book with poems that everyone will like, however some are contentious, or quite complex intellectually and thus they had to be strategically placed further into the volume.

One will come to understand why the title of this book is *Mélange*, a word borrowed from geology signifying a confusing but interesting mixture.

Table of Contents

Things That Are

Mélange	1
The Poetry of I	2
Weird Head	2
Ignorance	3
Robespierre Redux	4
Evil	5
American Vipers	6
Gun Nuts	7
Stupidity Embraced	8
The Torch and Pitchfork Brigade	9
A Ride on the Sorry Side	10

What Has Passed

Poetry of Blood	11
Lists of the Slaughtered	12
Death of the Artist	13
A Gift So Dear	14
Unrequited	15
Anna Laura	16

Somber And Melancholy

October Sky	17
My Saddest Song	17
Martha	18
Passing a Looking Glass	20
The Wisp	20
Tear Drops on File	21
Susurrus	22
Wander On My Love	23
Empty	23
Linger in Destiny's Arms	24

That Which Remains

Morning	25
A Woodcock Ascends	25
Reverie	26
The Farm Walker	27
The Wreck in the Meadow	28
The Old Millpond	30
The Wood Pile	30
The Water Trough	32
Tom	33
Morning in Contrast	34

A Gargantuan Struggle

The Algorithm Blues	35
Applied Quantum Mechanics	36
Annihilation	36
De Rerum Natura	38
Paradigmatic Reflection	39
Intransigent Phenomenology of Ignorance or Dumbing It Down	40
Excruciating Tremor	41

THINGS THAT ARE

Mélange

It came in a dream
orange in color
and I awoke in pain
A demand that I
collect the remnants
of my tired mind
That pesky muse
I want to devour
forces them out
A collection devolved
from I know not where
She squeezes them
from deep recesses
of an addled brain
into manila folders
I am done
Empty

The Poetry of I

Nothing but I
or sometimes me
Scan the pages
of modern verse
encounter trivia,
every thing trite
white on white
lacking insight
The editing pen
scrubs it clean

Weird Head

Alas, I awoke with a weird head
My mind declared it to be Sunday
but fact declared it Wednesday
Trite anxieties flared and raged,
sputtering like water on a hot griddle
My synapses were short-circuiting
Imagery that challenged sanity
Vexing malfunctions were anticipated
Rigid concepts shattered
A humble glass habitually accepted
insisted on meticulous definition
The conventional became absurd
with reality a poriferous fog,
all an annoying discombobulation

Ignorance

Civilization's disease
mutates into diverse factions
Its guises are many
Myth its cloak
Superstition its vehicle
Conspiracy its fertilizer
Into the minds of the masses
blinding the eyes of reason,
it is deceptive
for the bearer is ignorant
of its affliction
It creates faith,
energizes its growth
like a benevolent malignancy
It hosts a frightful weapon
wielded clandestinely,
dousing enlightenment,
causing darkness
wherein its spores thrive
like mold in a cave

Robespierre Redux

Vultures circle a road kill
Smug covetous accumulators
carry all to the tree top
Weed seeds in their dung
trickle down upon the soil
creating tentacles that suck out
the nutrients of human happiness
forming fruit for the very few
We rise to whack them down,
yet inevitably they return
spouting righteous piety
preaching convoluted rightness
and perverted logic to justify
their pestilent existence

Time again for the guillotine's
raspy fall and thump
Convert yachts and wealth hovels
to hope for the common man
Ah, read in folly's tattered pages
the tiresome cycle of lessons
taught and never learned
Trampled peasant revolts
countless revolutions
the Reign of Terror
soar like rockets
into civilization's darkest nights
Wat Tyler lives

Evil

A curious little word,
four letter words,
hate being kindred ,
tend to be nasty,
bad in the superlative
Small but mighty
germinating powerful
visceral concepts
that seize souls
with blackness of spirit
perverse rationality
fills the air
with phrenetic pathogens
spreading with
incremental velocity
infecting minds,
creating fiery zealots,
destroying civility,
leaving kindness
a torn garment
upon the floor

American Vipers

Presented a microphone,
millions as remuneration,
thence with voracious ignorance,
endowed with profligate stupidity,
bearing life stories of vile banality,
they disgorge their pernicious myth
of inviolable heroic superiority
of perceived rightful dominance,
feeding fear to the frightened mob

Abusive to common sensibility
they spew ignorance and hate
out of their rancid prejudice,
an America of violence,
anti- intellectualism its creed
No one asserts more certitude
than a person knowing nothing
Paranoia the vital nutrient
feeding fantasies of conspiracy
promoting wicked elfin phantoms
keeping minds free of reality

How big a word is hate,
as small as xenophobia
They be cowards one and all,
each dodged the service draft,
shunned brave athletic endeavor,
thus warriors only in their dreams
Power through loquacity,
belligerently promoting undue fear,
exhorting malevolence for avarice
leaders in perversion of rationality

Gun Nuts

Machine fed fervor
throwing pieces of lead
where ideas should go
Icons of ignorance with
crotch grabbing primeval urges
Primordial instincts stimulate
innate aggressive responses
Primal fears grounded in the soil
embellished with specious myth
Meat for the table
the enduring fable

A sickness awarded honor
Lunatics most fervent,
those demanding most
should have the least
They protest raucously,
a chorus of the frightened,
their shouts demean reason
Rampant paranoia
conjures conspiracies
Enemies with fright
like children in the night

Fiery lust from those
who least deserve trust
Words from these affrighted
proclaim to protect,
provide rancorous safety
from terrors yet to be seen
Exerting masculine power
explosive metal phalluses
puncture our tender flesh
Blood and lead their statement,
the gentle caress of the beast

The pomposity of argument,
lacking credulity of worth
proclaim a paean of freedom,
liberty under a hammer,
cowardice under the guise
of twisted patriotism,
petulant haughty pride
whence masculine anger boils
projecting lead spitted venom
True warriors shun bravado,
their bravery quiet and innate

Stupidity Embraced

Smiling tarts prevail
Barstool philosophers reign
Anti-intellectualism
the mobs narcotic
Witness verbal alchemy
where reason permutes,
commuting brilliant to dull
buffing dumb to sparkle
Jeer the superb mind,
throw it deep into the pool
where it sparkles unseen,
spit on the glittering ripples
Burnish the lie, abrade the truth
Sing the masses a simple song
Dizzy glib tongued babes,
fat smirking millionaires,
idiots muttering inanities
while they are hurrahed
The snake came
and Eve bit the apple
and Adam smiled
They lie, they lie
and we can only sigh

The Torch and Pitchfork Brigade

Again we can hear the call
a gentle rolling lulling murmur
a slow mourning breeze
that rustles dead newspapers
on our filthy sleeping streets
Ah, that moan that awakens
the slumbering masses
Whispers sprout seeds
that burst into shouts
Small shuffling steps growing,
becoming a heavy rhythmic tread
Once again torch flames reflect,
dancing in angry eyes
Moral outrage throbs within
yesterday's placid souls
fermenting pulsating migraine agony
inseminated while witnessing
brazen blind immune stupidity,
an addicted mob worshiping
icons of lofty privilege,
enjoying a reverence for ignorance
satiated and placated by dribble,
scraps dropped by paeans of greed
We finally awaken with a foot
upon our starved parched throats
Listen as of yore
Once again light the torches

A Ride on the Sorry Side
The Number 8 Bus

The Metro cruises the streets
its platform reaching out
like a mechanical reptile tongue,
slow and grumbling,
to raise chairs and walkers
of a city's downtrodden load,
heavy, infirm, and destitute
Their every chore major labor,
the sadness of exiguity,
declares pity a useless notion
as reality is hardened beyond
condescension of conscience
Too much, too much
A bus ride through
a mean existence
while investment banks
run their power algorithms
churning gigantic paper profits,
generating obscene bonuses
for arrogant pirates of commerce
They too have their rides,
private planes to luscious estates
and ever bigger yachts
The obscenity of comparative contrast
shakes the temperate soul
dampening any passion of hope
as poor people's coins
jangle into the collector

THINGS THAT PASS

Poetry of Blood

Bosnian Serb poet Radovan Karadzic
to be tried for war crimes including genocide

the fiend is a poet
an artisan of verse
and an ethic cleanser
finding pleasure in tormenting souls
seeing beauty in rivers of blood
hearing music in the screams of rape
creating genocide sung in poetry
long ago garlanded by a Bishop
in his masterly *The Mountain Wreath**

visualize semantics of ritual murder
where cruelty reigned supreme
found deep within the depths
of heartless negative compassion
with massacres honored as victories
where hatred grows like wildflowers
in a farmer's fallowed field
where some welcome beauty,
others see rapacious weeds

extermination is total victory
cruelty executed most supremely
pious sanity of the righteous
devoted followers of the deity
who injected primitive dogma
into an ancient peasant's mind
oh, we cry for the nobility wrung
from a wretched poet's soul,
perverting lyricism to sing of death

*A classical poem written in 1846 by Bishop Petar II Petrovic Njegos about a Christmas Eve massacre of hundreds of Muslims, an event inspired by another bishop, Bishop Danilo.

Lists of the Slaughtered

*And some there be which
have no memorial, who
are perished as though
they had never been.*
Ecclesiasticus 44:9

An ode to nothingness
out of complex being
Naught is as vacuous
as having never been
unless you have been
and are now as nothing,
random atoms afloat
in the vast universe
Some we cannot know
because you flicked
and perished hardly seen,
and then there are those
included in huge totals
on bureaucratic lists
where existence was lost,
extinguished into the ether
with a futile last breath

Death of the Artist

They all die, everyone does
However, some walk special
Just like you my compassionate friend,
gracing the streets with your presence,
illuminating the world with your art.
You have left a corporeal vacancy
and a rich wonderful residuum,
great fine art, the immortal gift,
a long lifetime of effortless kindness.
Memories of a wonderful person,
our tenacious task to cherish and keep
We will miss you, yet we have you

to Bob Solotaire
October 2008

A Gift So Dear

Him so very near,
innocent and content
we waited
He did not come
Hear my futile cry,
my muffled sobs,
our dream took flight
A gap opened in my heart
larger than all of space
Only dried tears remain

Now let me state
a golden promise
extended pure and perfect
from the baby's love
We will hold it very tight,
cherish his gift forever
It is that which remains
where it all began
Therein is what matters,
the seeds to a future
where happiness
will once again breathe
in sparkling sunlight

                to my wonderful friend Gabriel upon the
                loss of her newborn baby Jack, May 2012

Unrequited

Sing a plaintive song of need,
seeking succor the boy encounters torment
Tranquil leaves whisper gentleness
where averred mercy hovers
Alas, upon groomed acres below evil lurks

Fever long ago obliterated his hearing
Now assigned to a idyllic haven refuge
a caregiver's evil lust
assaulted his tender spirit
smashing the young man's soul,
his screams mute in the esteemed school

While policemen's itchy fingers
twitched upon rifle triggers
bewildered he pled with the world
to understand, to assuage his agony
He spoke hand sign language
asking the world to please listen
to a tale of afflicted misery,
to share the plight of all who suffer

With raging authority
restrained by a fine thread
large aroused armed men
released a fusillade of bullets
through the air to dance into his chest
Bureaucrats approve a job well done
Violence now officially sanctioned,
another notch upon their trophy wall
But the tears still flow ebbing
into a pool that never dries
as we ask where justice resides

> For my friend George Levier.
> Police murdered his physically
> and emotionally handicapped
> brother James on March 16, 2001

Anna Laura

Ancient black and white photo
beside Lake Owassa,
perhaps 1946 the year
My father's mother
with warm kind smile
caught in perpetuity
I search for memories
Smell her fresh baked bread
As hospital board president
giving children red rubber balls,
our first after the war
As board of education president
she joins patriotic songs
beside the victory garden
at our one room school
She reads the leaves
at the bottom of a tea cup
and tells the future
Her milk pitcher collection
fills a room with beauty
I study the picture
trying to remember
this robust woman
to enjoy her character
knowing it was good
The funeral director
said her service
his largest ever
and that tells it all

> Anna Laura Pierson, née Rancier
> Wife of Foster, Sr.
> Born 1887 – died 1947

Somber And Melancholy

October Sky

Sophistry abounds in the eye
An unripe peach is but a promise
A sky full of whipped cream,
cumulative giant joyful mounds
Greedy attempts to lick it all up
but the tongue flops to earth
as a rug thrown over a line
Vanity corrupts all that you see
A large blue hole I would jump through
landing upon where it does not matter
A reason to fail is a friend not here
So lusty spittle through the hole
blows back in a ferocious gale
My tear riding an updraft crystallizes
salt seasoning the crisp clean air
I mutter about patterns that do not hold

My Saddest Song

I wrote a love song
for a man to sing
in hope a sweetheart
to me it would bring
Many a pretty girl I have met,
but she is the prettiest yet

Oh, as the night grew long
he sang my plaintive song
What affect that tune did make,
many a heart it will surely break
My intended sweetheart,
she did deeply sigh
Indeed, not an eye
in that crowd was dry

I am not a happy guy
No need to wonder why
My pretty girl, she did fall
for the singer across the hall
Singing my song he soared
with her blissfully aboard
I a little wiser, a lot sadder
She, the prettiest I have met,
lost to the best verse
I have written yet

Martha

A hard flame to kindle
Her name like America,
homemade cherry ice cream
and warm colonial things

Hundreds of words not said
all lost in fantasy's bed
Futile mutterings to specters
cavorting about in my night
Desire that we come together,
obstinate fantasies again and again
I fear a polarity of our souls,
dissimilar wants that will not meet

We fools write poems of love
Vain efforts throughout time,
scribblings that do not survive
Yet foolishly we try again
Search for why-
      her name
      the girl
      some need
      something

What is time to one man's loneliness,
careening desire, boiling love,
lust described as passion
Concentrate and compress
Make it a tiny grain of sand
from the cosmic beach
where wash the waves
of our emotional eternity

Through the dark night -
    I cry
    I scream
    I lust
As so many before
Ridiculous in rationality
Other eyes appraise
impugning her assigned purity,
tearing me apart internally

I love a girl named Martha
There it is actually exclaimed,
whispered a thousand times
Write a sonnet if you want
about counting the ways
All that matters is stark reality -
she does not love me
we will not exist
I plead to time to let tenses slip
into the comfort of memory
I loved a girl named Martha,
her name was like America -
myths of certainty
of what should be
homemade cherry ice cream

1966

Passing a Looking Glass

A pathetic old fool
caught in a mirror
quite by chance
Quite an encounter,
a frightening event
Uncovering sad truth
like an old love letter
forgotten in dusty drawer
A vision suspected
yet never acknowledged
Stark vivid reality
viewed from outside in
The graffiti of age
rudely disfigures
an unclouded page
Perhaps mistaken
There is no chance

The Wisp

A wrenlet darts around
an ancient gnarled oak
A wisp of a breeze
brings in the muse
changing thoughts to art
bemusing a person,
flirting with fate
tantalizing the soul
Pleasure becomes agony
Her smile melts ice
Ethereal is not real
but the muse plays
that it is genuine

Always there and gone
Converts pleasure
to teasing torment
Muses are playful
tempting a weak mortal
beguiling the ardent fool
It is what muses do
Coveting artists desire all
knowing this cannot be
Not to be possessed
lighthearted wile
provokes desire
connoting happiness
that cannot be

Passion runs rampant
You love things
you cannot have
Ah the wretchedness
Excise her pesky being
and there is naught
Creation has its price
Residue is in the art

to Katie

Tear Drops on File

Those happy days begot lovers
laughing as they ran wildly
with hair blowing in the wind
We cannot forget eyes
that searched for love,
joyful common discovery
Now all of that begets
the saddest memories

I leaf slowly back
through the pages of my mind
marking with flickering smiles
heads tossing upon pillows,
heart sparked pangs of regret,
love used and devoured

Pages pasted together
in happy splashes
yellowed by time
saved for happy recall
Now the worst, the very worse,
that dreaded memoir
of love forever passed,
kindling deep melancholy

Susurrus

The sadness departed,
chased by you
a wisp of smoke
riding a gentle breeze.
No enjoyment in misery
nor solace in tears
Disquiet eased,
troubles resolved
with you involved
Your ethereal caress,
felicity resides
A wound without a scar

Wander On My Love

I hear the breeze whisper
I can see it gently rustle
the grass and leaves
as it eases through
into the celestial sphere
where all such collect
Her breath is stilled
taken by that breeze
as a spirit on a quest
Perchance the constancy
of things that never cease

Empty

Our messages arrive
within empty envelopes
There are no words
Niceties begging utterance
choke inside the mind
Trivial bits become
leaden particles
when immense worry
muffles the brain
Uncertainty mutes
our casual voice
We cannot whisper
when screams
need to be heard

Linger in Destiny's Arms

Take me back to choose and enjoy
abundant fruit on a luscious tree
A deity gave Adam a warning
Chance presented me opportunity
Woefully I did not pause to linger
but rushed through the garden
as though there are always other days
With a piteous longing sigh
I recall abundance and variety
Beauty inclines to be effervescent
leaving behind delightful sensations,
insistence its evanescing command
Ah to go back to nullify the perfidy
of careless expended moments,
to again savor libidinous sensuality,
to be intoxicated with passion
to linger and enjoy and perchance
be ensnared where I should have stayed

That Which Remains

Morning

On a chilled autumn morning
viewed from the warmth of my bed,
alone in the dark blue predawn sky
perfectly framed by a window square
glows the welcome bright morning star

Not a star at all but the planet Venus
reflecting light from a rising sun
Each day gives infinite promise
to all before and all to come
What is, has been, and will be

A Woodcock Ascends

She rose before the sun
to step to the great beyond,
into the gray sadness
That might be nowhere
yet something might be
Alas, we fear a dark nothing
We send a whispered message,
a futile plea to let us know

As we walk the wood
a woodcock explodes
through the brightening sky
into the chill air
It pauses a brief moment
to hover before our eye
then quietly glides away,
having proffered an answer
we embrace with solemnity

Reverie

on pondering what
has been long pondered
the significance
of redoing the obvious
seeking profundity where
countless predecessors
did the unceasing same
watching tired waves
crash on ancient rocks

reflected golden sun
fractures away on
the undulating surface
a seabird effortlessly glides
through splashed foam
as if to signal
a trenchant answer
to something not a question

transcendence is found
in being present
where contemplation
is blithely generated
to finally end
an emptied shell
dropped back
by a screaming gull
into a persistent sea

upon the Maine coast

The Farm Walker

I walk though endless fields,
farms that were once here,
my legs shambling through
lush wheat and rye grass,
past copses and bramble thickets,
patches set aside by kind nature.

I walk luxurious green carpets
that ramble over the far horizon
into damp copious meadows
where milk cows might look up
as they slowly browse and chew
The horses erect, ears arise alert
until they consider all is safe

There are wire fences to pass
and fieldstone walls to climb
Wildflowers and errant berries
inhabit the fence rows where
song birds flit and glide about
Floating and hopping insects
perambulate in particular ways

Mine an ancient lonesome trek
enjoying a solitary quality,
a place of changeless peace,
a glance at perfect forever,
planted in the furrows of memory
known only to the farm walker

The Wreck in the Meadow

A liquor delivery truck
failed the sharp turn
by Sherrill's lush meadow
early one spring morning.
That a quiet sleepy place
with a tiny meandering brook
rife with frogs and watercress.
Scattering across the wet green
flew bottles of every brand.
Heifers grazed undisturbed
looking on with bovine disdain.
A morning shift of workers
commuting to a nearby mill
gazed in credulous wonder,
awed by this dream come true.

Sherrill finished morning milking
ready to accept whatever event,
anything to disrupt a farmer's day.
His a primitive farm, ancient machines,
iron wheeled wagons, and draft horses.
He scratched a hard living from
patches of green on thin soil
beneath limestone escarpments.
The shaken truck driver waits
with hands on his head,
this not to be his best day.
Eagerly entreated by opportunists
declaring this indeed a blessed event,
he reconciles to inherent affability,
telling all to help themselves.

Thus does destiny sway and turn
The sleepy meadow soon picked clean,
songbirds and damselflies flit about.
The mill's day shift is soon sent home,
their drunken revelry a legend born.
Sherrill too harvests this bounteous crop
gathering arm loads of bottles to
cache in dusty nooks and crannies,
behind beams, in hay lofts and feed bins,
through the rambling old red barn.

As a farmer's work is never done
he had never tasted demon rum.
Now with opportunity presented
a latent thirst was awakened.
A wary righteous wife stood guard
diligently alert to evil inherent
from such easy dubious bounty.
Nevertheless, he imbibed regularly
sampling from this ample reserve.
She never knew to pull a cord
hanging from the water trough
attached to a bottle deep within.
Old age crept in like an autumn frost
while tired joints and muscles
were ritually lubricated by a gift,
tonic delivered unexpectedly
on a long ago spring morn.

In a joyous postscript,
we tore down that old barn
many years, aye decades, hence.
We found dusty remainders
and will attest that if anything,
those brews improved with age.
We hoisted a drink, or two, to ole Sherrill,
a tired farmer and a damned good man.

The Old Millpond

Ah, the poignant ecstasy
the hot sweaty body
fresh from dusty haying
or the long distance run
drops into the cold depths
Eyes look up in defiance
toward the midday sun
Cold to the exact point
before pleasure escapes
one treads water
feeling the cool kneading
while inquiring minnows
nibble the distant toes
A damselfly hovers
pausing and darting
With all sides embraced
by forbidding vegetation
the pond has constancy
refusing the extremes -
winter's full cover of ice
summer's relentless heat

The Wood Pile

A persistent mass of short sawed logs
always present in the back lot
awaiting what my father determined
to be an idle child seeking good labor
The result of trees felled the previous year
Logs drawn out by straining horses
to meet the large whirling circular saw,
cutting lengths suitable for stove and hearth

Perfect hockey ice beckoned,
Books waited to be read
A blond haired girl at the next farm
Unexplored woods and fields taunted,
but the woodpile stood undiminished
Axes, a splitting maul, sledgehammer, wedges,
heavy cold steel, there always ready for work

Some of the cut rounds,
red oak, maple, beech
surrender and split with ease
Birch, apple, pine, soft and gentle
All welcome my arching lofty hard blow
awarding that pleasant small satisfaction
achieved through victory over small things

Alas, as in life there are knots,
where one meets up with resistance,
requiring a driven wedge or two to confront
the innate perversity of inanimate objects
One day all our elms died and joined the pile
They did not go gentle into the good stove,
their structure gnarled and stringy,
the essence of innate cantankerousness
Tangled fibers grabbed and swallowed
maul and sledge driven wedges
causing a flow of bad words into the good air

Ah, there was pure goodness in that labor,
constructing well split stacked cords
from an indomitable pile that never shrank
It was good hard rhythmic labor
in cold bracing country air defying
all the laws of thermodynamics

The Water Trough

Standing here in the future
a magnificent urban artifact
where horses drank long ago
An imposing granite monument
amidst parking meters aligned
where hitching posts once stood
Large troughs on three sides
catch water in constant flow
while on the backside a tiny spout,
perchance a relative significance,
flows for human indulgence

Rhythmically clopping on cobble stones
farmers' wagons and carriages
from distant farm and town estates
joined trolley horses from city streets,
draft teams from the nearby firehouse,
all twitching and snorting,
tails swatting at nagging flies,
enjoying respite and cool comfort,
equitable in their basic need,
cold clear water quenching thirst

Now, more than a century since,
those scurrying by do not note
that which remains steadfast here
Occasionally horses pulling tourists
receive a cool welcome respite,
a gift from the long ago past
Wicket this hot summer day
drinks from a lower aperture
knowing it special for thirsty dogs
In the evening a homeless woman
bathes in the clean coolness,
a welcome kindness unforeseen
one hundred years in the past

Federal Street
Portland, Maine

Tom

Big, black, sharp eyed rooster,
each morning he stretches
above the horse barn flock,
silhouetted against blue Georgia sky
letting loose a sounding cry
across the field to handsome Gilly
and his goat barn flock.
In chorus they awaken a farm

Valiantly he protected his hens
against a formidable Red-tailed hawk.
Now, on a foggy Sunday morn
he fights a crafty fox
coveting the panicked hens.
With raging defensive fury
he hurls talons at the creature
in a struggle he cannot win.
Finally, torn and broken he lies
prostrate upon the henhouse floor

Gabriel stares down in grief
at the frightful loss of her
big beloved Ameraucana,
so very brave and protective.
Wait! A spark still glows!
He raises his head and crows.
She gently carries him off
in her loving nursing hands.

Wounded Tom sore and healing
stands now back on guard
above his clucking flock.
A heroic faithful sentinel,
alert eyes turned toward
the ominous far dark wood.

Morning in Contrast

first light is hope
another chance
perchance subsist
in a better day

vexing counterpoint
of my existence
'tween being here
or being there

with clangs and bangs
a city awakens rough,
screaming pigeons and gulls
fight over bread crusts

with nature murmuring
a farm emerges gentle,
from where the hens roost
a rooster calls arise

a farm comes forth
denoting simplicity
the city arises sluggish
venerating complexity

the city opens aurally
we hear its pulse
a steady crescendo
of spirited endeavor

upon the vibrant farm
we absorb the known,
the sun a metronome
setting the day's pace

night, the city anthropic
collapses with a gasp,
within nature's province
things gently bed down

A Gargantuan Struggle

The Algorithm Blues

Got them algorithm blues
Thumping technological news
Squirming little parasites upon
the fleas that bite the dog
Billions of bytes of data
and me, and you, just bits,
corpuscles in the body economic
Thousands of math geeks,
their pasty fingers upon buttons,
feed and churn every possible fleck
into massive copulating equations
that strip away our nonobjectivity,
depreciating nuance, voiding humanity
Empiricism rules, inseminating
the gangling computer models
Humans reduced to data pods
Thoughts dreams ideas converted
into utilitarian statistical mush
A black hole that sucks in privacy
converting it to market feed
It crushes our layered simulacra
into a singular utilitarian form,
fertilizing the insatiable marketplace
Ah the incessant electrical humming
of those sad algorithm blues that
shake freedom's willful essence
where even tears are collected,
registered, processed and projected

Applied Quantum Mechanics

History's rhythms ride the waves of time
Find comfort in the constancy of discord
Lo, old triumphs generate inconsequential
transforming to odious worn memories
Dreams only seductive synapse impulses
Lament the lost surge of youthful optimism
For just one fleeting moment we shine
like a sun caught single piece of quartz
on a vast expanse of sandy beach,
itself beautiful for the fact of its composite
Beware the tyranny of randomness,
probability an opiate to the hopeful
Futility is not to be found in having existed,
aye, the plaintive cry is imbued in that once is all
Truth being each minute becomes incrementally less,
yet, there is satisfaction in the quantum process

Annihilation

Walk about knowing
they are there everywhere,
mechanisms of transmission
cell phones, radios, satellites
dutifully emanating electrons
all pulsating and emitting
digital and analog formats
flitting about and streaming by
The trite and the meaningful,
intimate conversations impact
and we cannot feel or hear
We know they fill the air
swirling around and through,
invisible gusts of verbiage
descending somewhere into
an instrument of reception

Venture to Plato's cave
guided by sage Socrates
blind one's thinking self
experience another reality,
listen to the shadows on the wall
Practice secular aniconism,
shun the graphic image
They are truly there,
these hypothetical waves,
free in Aristotle's ether,
what he thought was something
but it is nothing but nothing

Now see the unseen
shift the polarity of reality
We are engulfed within
spatial spirals and convolutions
winding about us like endless
black strands of spaghetti
composed of electric ions
They striate the infinite ether
randomly bounce and careen
converting to fixed rhythms

Flip a cosmic circuit
break the connectives,
the bits flutter and fall
a lifeless black snow
of no purposeful utility,
all of cognition neutralized
into nonfunctional particles
The electron defeated,
a cyber catastrophe
No sound but silence
except when the expanding
cosmos hisses and roars

De Rerum Natura
On the Nature of Things

The atom exists
wrote poet Lucretius
two millennia ago
He knew it existed,
not what it is.
It was always there,
always will be
Nothing produces nothing,
cannot produce nothing
so there is something
Fortuna made it him

Dangerous idea
to be basic material
Incompatible as we fear
raging angry gods,
haters of pleasure
Monks aghast hid it
behind a rigid
wall of ignorance
until rescued by
Poggio Florentinus

Innumerable atoms
collide randomly in space
forming complex structures,
that revert to atoms
We from celestial seed
whence all evolve
last not forever
Only atoms are infinite

Epicurus saw results
sans hierarchal confines
Machiavelli to Montaigne
to Newton and Darwin
Jefferson and Einstein
Atomists all finding pleasure
in knowing the secret
of the ancient light
Dust to dust

Paradigmatic Reflection

Sitting upon a bench in the little green park
I find around me a muddle of concave mirrors
each emitting an utterance laden with certainty
The whole a confusing dialectical syntagma,
a rousing paradiddle of marching truths,
polarities bounce about like table tennis balls
Simulacrums worn like veils of armor
decorated with modern coats of arms,
status symbols of mercantile trade,
determine to be different but are identical
We profess similarity within our species,
however constancy is found above
with the oak leaves, sparrows, and bees

Intransigent Phenomenology of Ignorance or Dumbing It Down

Complexity shunned as if stars
are but twinkling crystals
Lies, lies, lies are those stars in the sky
Simplicity the craved diet pill
purging the fat of thought
File down the apex of intellect,
eliminate all height and depth,
toss its flaccid form, a fait accompli
upon the common floor
Ah, the bovine stares, the barstool philosophers,
babbling, blabbing, blathering, nattering,
satiated frontal lobes emitting satisfied grunts
Societal dysfunction oozes forth
from a sweet pabulum mental diet
Anti-intellectualism a credo served up
as slops in a hog trough
Supernatural creeds pound down spikes of reason
driving them beneath the plebeian surface
into a battered trash bin of wisdom
where they are never to be seen,
banished from human selectivity,
a grave trod on by a heavy jackboot
molded of profane human ignorance
Yes, a polite cover for indigenous stupidity

Excruciating Tremor

These are not pleasant sounds
assaulting our reluctant ears
and provoking pitiable tears,
a steady beat of cries, whimpers,
and horrific screams menacing
our persisting innocent dreams

What species is this,
what raging bloody foul creation?
Can incrementalism be applied,
a varied depth of revulsion
to raging indiscriminate slaughter,
loathsome bloodletting hatred
denying rational description,
to cold vacant morality
that leads to lopping off limbs,
wanton rape of women and children,
selling women into sexual slavery,
permitting rape and sale of children,
stealing the food of the starving,
shredding cultures for coins,
creating child warriors?

Is there a quality to be found
in killing without torment?
Can humanity's senses be so dulled,
awareness of outrage so benign
that we can be at ease,
can nod in acknowledgement
that we can smile and enjoy
our resplendent consuming trivia
while begging pleas for mercy,
excruciating screams of terror,
death chortles rend this planet's air,
an element that we share?

These are not pleasant sounds
assaulting our reluctant ears

About the Author

Duane Robert Pierson's early schooling was in a one-room schoolhouse with no plumbing, no electricity. He was awarded a Bachelor of Arts in biology and history from the University of Alabama, and a Master of Science and Doctor of Philosophy from Cornell University.

He has been an executive, a teacher and professor, an infantry officer, athlete, art gallery owner, stonemason, farmer, photographer, and always a poet.

Books by Duane Robert Pierson
Published by Integritas Publishing
Portland, Maine

On Reviving a Lost Revolution: *Poetry*

Ode to Frieda: *Poetry*

When Young Men Die: *Poetry of War*

Frogs, Dogs, and Eclogues: *Poetry, Rural and Pastoral*

Field of Wildflowers with Girl: *Poetry of Love, Romance, and Related Confusion*

When My Feet Quit Dancing: *Poetry on the Personal Side*

The Indictment: *Poetry Most Critical*

Mélange: *Poetry*

Annie and The Prince of Wales - *An Historical Novel*

PORTLAND PUBLIC LIBRARY SYSTEM
5 MONUMENT SQUARE
PORTLAND, ME 04101

MAY 29 2014

WITHDRAWN